THE MINNOW WOULD BE LOST

Nora Chassler was born in Madison, Wisconsin, in 1972, and grew up in New York City. She has an undergraduate degree in English from Hunter College, CUNY, in New York, and a Masters in Creative Writing from St Andrews. She has worked as a model and a social worker. She lives in Edinburgh.

Her first novel, *Miss Thing*, was published by Two Ravens Press in 2010. Her second, *Grandmother Divided by Monkey Equals Outer Space*, was published by Valley Press in 2015. A collection of 'fragments, pensées and table-talk' titled *Madame Bildungsroman's Optimistic Worldview* followed in 2017.

The Minnow
Would Be Lost

NORA CHASSLER

Valley Press

First published in 2020 by Valley Press
Woodend, The Crescent, Scarborough, YO11 2PW
www.valleypressuk.com

ISBN 978-1-912436-30-9
Cat. no. VP0150

A CIP record for this book is available from the British Library.

Cover design by Jamie McGarry.
Text design by Peter Barnfather.

Printed and bound in Great Britain by
Imprint Digital, Upton Pyne, Exeter.

Contents

In loving memory of Cordelia Bradby

'When, striving for access to the word and to time, she identifies with the father, she becomes a support for transcendence. But when she is inspired by that which the symbolic order represses, isn't a woman also the most radical atheist, the most committed anarchist? In the eyes of this society, such a posture casts her as a victim. But elsewhere?'

—Julia Kristeva, *About Chinese Women*

The Proem

Gilligan.[1]

Red shirt, white cap
All threat removed

Castration does that

I can't spell. I never could

What saves me is the simple truth
It'll be the same for you

Such unities
Of time, character and event
Are best on sitcoms

Aristotle would have clapped
Aristotle would have clap pity
Clap pity clap clapped[2]
In front of
A live studio audience
And from deep
Within it

Some demands just must be met

And then—

Shop shut. Shop shut!
You swallowed the plot
Hook line

And sinker

Piss off!
We haven't got any milk
Shop shut.

Poor Gilligan

He wasn't gay
He wasn't asexual

Castrated, in any event,
And a castaway

Always had the same shirt on,
Like me and you

That was necessary

He was the fearless crew

Now who's confused?

This could be
In any order
Go back

Go back[3]

1. The Lyric

I started to tell you this thirty years ago
You turned away with a 'sulky gesture of refusal'
I was fourteen,
You couldn't've been too much more than ten
Just a child[4]
Remember how we fought?
This is all your fucking fault

Just passing through?
… But you're not *dressed*
for a wedding…[5]

> *Itheherome widens his rheumy*
> *eyes*

O … It's The Journey that you want
With cash and prizes[6] at the end
Shiver me timbers and
Sit the hell down then
I can't grab your legs and bend.
Four legs, two legs, three
Crawls, walks, talks

Shites itself, and dies
The Sphinx had an ass for a face[7]
Oedipus my ass

Remember Sandra Bernhard
Kidnapping Jerry Lee Lewis
In *The King of Comedy*?
She makes this romantic dinner

And Jerry's mouth
Is taped shut

The crystal chandelier
Over their two-top

The sound of crystals
Hitting each other

Sound like water
And *look* like water

The sun hitting the Hudson
Millions of crystal arrowheads

                    Henry Hudson. Bad man.
                    Floating after the mutiny
                    In what is now called
                    Hudson Bay
                    Starving to death
                    Floating around
                    In a rowboat

Picture the dark hallway
Below the hallway
In your tenement
Between the stairs
And the other stairs
The one to the basement—
Mouse shit, branches, old hair

I was a rotten lad
But you, you were my petal
You were my petal

I'm no' really here
I just said that
To put you at your ease
I'm only type, and beads.
Remember me?

That corpse
You dreamed about
Overcoat,
Tasseled scarf,
Hook nose, Jew.[8]

He was standing in the hall
Between the garden stair
'Under the yellow pet shop'
That ends with your front door

You look like you might puke.
The smell of my old jute purse
Or me?
Moss and resin, beard and cumin.
Sit still, man!
We sure were
Brought up badly.

Here are the gems

Itheherome takes crystals from his
pocket. His fingernails are long and dirty;
he lays the stones on a tea towel that's
cut from the same cloth as his plaid shirt

Which do you wanna hold?

Rose Quartz?
Of course, of course
I could tell by your acne scars you're a sap.

Come, on! That's OK. We're friends
For now, anyway.
My favorite? How strange …
That you consider me.
I'll tell you later. To start
Let's conjure—who? Choose.
Rumi?
Really?
Your wish is my command.

I think he was pished, rat-arsed, don't you?
We can't know, you and I.
Always on the garden path[9]
And why

A red tulip for the stealin'
A red wagon for the chasin'[10]
Mine was so small
I had to crawl
Everything I had was toy-sized
In those days
I was a child
Though already six foot ten
I wore a uniform
I wore a boiler suit

My wagon was wayyyy too small

Maybe the dark hallway?
Below the entrance to your tenement
Between the stairs
And the other stairs

I absolutely love to sleep.
Eschewing booze
I exercise at dawn.
When the sky is dark
And sun is gone
I dreamed of this place long ago

I also knew the earth was round
(and slightly squished)
'The moment of engender'
However,
No sense trying to convince
Anyone of these things
Unless you're wanting stoned
Burned,
Whatever

For when I was a little girl.

These buildings weren't yet built, I dreamed
It was night, in the dream, it was dark
Floor-to-ceiling windows,
Watery blue at noon, gold was the light
Beside the Victorian cemetery

No curtains—no lace curtains

I liked them. I liked those net curtains
Auld dears had when we first came to Scotland.
Their scalloped edges
Finished, private, closed.
I miss the dated inside/outside split

Let's go back?
Let's go back.

Join me!
Chicago, 1973:
Two lice-ridden children
Eating burgers
At a greasy spoon
Living in a square
Brick house
A metal
Fence around the yard
Protecting one red tulip
Grown by the little girl.

A father pries
Lights from the bodies
Of fireflies, like those
Newborn turtles
The ones whose births
Are slow-mo catapults
In rows from out the
Skin
Of their mothers' backs

Our dad.

He put the torsos
On a spinning record
And the light made shapes[11]
Red, white and blue bows
Like postcards
Of time-lapse photos
Headlights and taillights
On every rotary rack
In every head shop
In NYC in the 1980s
O, how they span!

> *When girls were girls*
> *and men were men*
>
> *Mister we could use a man*
> *like Herbert Hoover again*
>
> *Didn't have no welfare state*
> *Everybody pulled their weight!*[12]

Meanwhile in the churchyard
The filmy baby-leaves
Loosely, shook it out

At the final call one chosen tow-head
Is chucked over the top step
Like a bag of mulch
Onto the stiff brown grass

It's always her
It's always the same fucking kid

'A gang of stupid racist white children'
From whom we were removed
Not a second too soon

I recall[13] the expired candy shop
Run by nuns with sweaty palms
And red long nails

The time-hardened 5 cent caramel
Twirled in its wax paper

One child in at a time

And the door shuts behind.

In order for our child bodies
To erase and simultaneously absorb
(Epigenetics—make note of that)
The horrifying events of the day

We jump on my bed
To the record *Help*
Lights out
In my own room. The last time
I had my own room—
Now it's a hostel—
No risk of my
Grabbing you tonight—
I sleep in a goddamned bunk bed
In a room full of bunk beds

And when we sleep
Time stops
I listened to the crickets
In the hot Chicago night,[14]
Inhale now

Itheherome inhales deeply

They sure as shit
Don't make smog
Or yellow smoke[15]
The way they used to

Visions are invited in
I'm dead cordial, do join me
For a tiny glass of Czech Becherovka

I was a charming little drunk in her own bed
Wise, long gone already
Hair the colour of Xerox paper
Stick your thumbnail
In the watery veil
Of the white rose petal
A black line appears
The strip of shit
In a cooked shrimp

A move East is made.

Phew! We outrun
The poor and stupid
Racist white children
Make the sleeper train
Out of Chicago.

You still *smoke*? Jesus.
I haven't had a cigarette
These twenty years.
I never liked
To hurt myself.

I was just addicted.
I suppose, to be fair
I liked to watch
                    the post-lung smoke
                                rising to the peeling ceiling
            or lowest branch

I was always odd, always saw
Up the tree's skirt
To the spine of your cradle
My mother said so,
And although she's in
The Guinness Book of World Records

For being the least
Reliable observer
Of all time
Ever

I believed
Her

Mutant, me.
Me, mutant.[16]
Is it my fault
I see the spiral
From within the spiral?

In this cemetery at dusk
The sun at its finest
Dream-angle
I can't believe all the things
You forgot

The nuns, the red light
Our dad
The red emergency
          button
In the elevator
The black buttons
The polished brass plate

It's not healthy
To repress so much, brother.

> *With silver buttons buttons buttons*
> *all down her back back back*
> *Miss Mary Mack Mack Mack*
> *all dressed in black black black*

My mother used to sing me that

I was writing a novel.
Followed the lass
From birth to death.
Madame Bildungsroman.[17]

During working hours
I crawled under
The fold-out picnic tables
In the sawdust

Living and dead beetles,
Used pipe cleaners
Spat-out fruit pips
Long human hairs

It all goes in my mouth

Pulling this tiny model
Of a covered wagon
Four hours, then lunch,
Then another four

The lunch was good
That nice dhal
The lad who made it
That's his stall

He's deid noo.

And sometimes when my reparations came
I treated myself
To a mango lassi

(Those have stopped, by the way
In case you were thinking
I'd increase your pay.)

I wrote it on a mobile
Eradicated any illusion
That we weren't
Just 'being here now'
I wrote the whole damn
Novel with my thumbs

It started with her birth.
Appalled by smells and language
The Lunatic Visceral
Then a 'shocking murder'
The Omniscient Narrator
Expressed surprise
All went tits up after that

Yeah.

This one had a phobia of birds
And that one had a phobia of bats
This one had six earrings climbing
This one ate no meat at all
Except Burger King
'Whalers'

Once we got to NYC

I began to look forward to TV

Particularly when
The storylines stopped
On Sesame Street and Mr. Rogers

I longed
For those puppetless
Interludes
The camera goes to a factory
Music in the background
Super 8 with fast hairs

Watch with me:
Lengthening ribbons of taffy
Colonnaded tin cans
Gentle, on metal tubes
Clipped wings of newspapers
Lifted by wire hands
Then tied with bows.

I want to talk about you now.

What have you been doing?

If you talk I can stop remembering the mosque.
How the breeze off the Hudson on Riverside
Blew the light curtains into the room
The previous tenant had soundproofed the walls
With bumpy grey foam that made my tongue shoot out
When I touched it by mistake
But out the window
How the River's wavelets
Lifted and dropped down like scales
In the Age of Fishes[18]

In Olden Days, waves were fish

Way before we were born
Matter and consciousness were one
Skin was tiles and beads was needs   *He laughs*
Before we spoke

A Sociopath

I stare into an old friend's husband's eyes
On the internet
Wondering if he was assigned
Female at birth
Even though he's got a beard
All the desire I have feels rooted in
The fact that I was assigned female
And it's so rubbish and it's so crap.

I've tried everything to feel good about it
But I feel weak and cheated, sexually.
I'm going to shove it all into this cupboard
Once I finish talking to you

And that's going to happen soon
You'll never see me again
I'm going back to an apartment that hasn't
Existed in forty years[19]
Slamming a door
Running up 13 flights of stairs in dirty
Fucking Pom Pom socks
My lungs full of wet courtyard and pigeon shit
And a hint of Pledge wood polish on the high breeze
Unpacking my case full of old dresses and face cream
My plastic necklaces
My desire for you that has haunted me these
Many years, this whole lifetime till I met you
Face to face; I couldn't *believe*
That's what you looked like this time
When you stood up from the picnic table

To greet me, your open *hi*, full of good faith
Finally. But now I see I made it all up
So I will put these feminine accoutrements of desire
Which I never liked much anyway
They reminded me of bowling
All that goddamned paraphernalia
And I was destined to suck?
Can't make the right posture,
Can barely lift the fucking ball
The food sucks, fuck hot dogs, no windows
Borrowed shoes!
In it all goes to the cupboard
I don't even need to lock it
The sheer weight of its contents keeps
The lid shut.

*

I detangled[20] my feelings
From any hope of deliverance—it took years
Everyday unpacking this bullshit line
And that; every fucking hour of
Every fucking day I dismantled us
And what we were meant to say

Passion brings suffering.
The happy ending is Reason's lackey.
Why can't anyone see this?
It's why we suffer.

Oh, you're all for Reason
Of course you are

Feel Reason in your body?
Too right you bloody don't.
It's the original virtual reality.
That's what Parmenides was saying.[21]
The Sun Goddesses at the gate to our yard

Command us:
'Go to bed for days and days'
I do. Every seasonal juncture, give or take,
They say I'm clinically depressed.
I get another ghost to man my stall

I beg to differ   *Itheherome is picking blonde*
                         hairs off his shirt. He isn't looking at you
                         anymore.

You'll start to feel again. Your body first, of course.

Insomniac? Of course. Of *course* you are.
And you only feel your body when you fuck.
Same old story
Most men are like that.

Oh well,
Whoops, and—sorry
"In front of the building,
but not in the lobby!"[22]

They thought it was OK to fuck kids
On loft beds and behind trees
Tell them God was dead
Me? Glad you asked
I think you should keep
Children in the dark.
You can always murder them
If you do something by accident
Or, what else?
The girl ones you can implant
A couple of rye seeds, those'll sprout
A filigree beneath her cheeks and underneath
You'll see that glow you love so well
And though that light hurts
All the fucking time
It is warm as a waffle iron
And keeps a hot stiffness in her face
Anticipatory and very attractive
Which leads to her ears when she smiles
Down the sides of her sore neck
Ski-jumps shoulders
To the outside of her ribs
Through her gut, on to her knees
Out the soles of her feet—
These connections once made
By whatever ley-line or train track
You tie the little kid to
And offer up as a sacrifice
To your dumb belief in purity—
Is permanent,

An initial investment, yes
But once it takes—

Sleeping during the day
No one can touch me

I love your sounds of work
I carry the pressure like a piano key

The moment before the sound

Held
Down

Wait, do you smell that?
Come on. Inhale.
Everything around here has smelled
Like a balloon
All morning. It's *weird*.

It's a braw mornin, is it?
9/11 weather. Wedgwood blue sky.

The desert has its charms.
Look at those giant clouds racing.
They look like chariots to me.
What about you? What do you see?
Or covered wagons on the prairie.

Everything we know about love
We learned from the animals

Humans are desperate desperate beasts
I don't know why

Oh, what the hell, I made you these
I felt too shy
To give you them
But now it's so pretty out
And what with the sky
Yes, what *are* they?
You did always get to the heart of things.
Little abstract mosaics, maybe?
I could make it into a key chain for you?
Yeah, give it a purpose
That would probably be better
For when you go home
I used old mirrors and shards of colored glass
Left after the bomb last year
Maybe the one the year before

The pieces are everywhere, if you only look
Here's a handful, under your foot
I like your boots.
They remind me of something.

The mosaic is a bit trinkety.
Abstract was boastful
I was never good at precision
I always had a lot of range.
Though very well behaved,
At times almost the teacher's pet
At times almost a sociopath[23]

For how my little sneaker itched to kick
Our quadrant of desks
Into a heap, climb it
And scream my white hair off
I could not believe
The task
Was to copy
Exactly
What was Written,
On the board
Already?

School's bad, isn't it?
Lunchrooms, humiliations
Someone's always about to punch you
Or already punching you
In the fucking face

And my mother's beady eyes picking me up
My mother's stoned crow's eyes, looking down
Brown as an old greasy mink
Whites like the whites of fried eggs
Above, the dark widow's peak
A headband like a riprap[24]
For her too-small skull
"Well, if you think so!'
Lips in a bow, she smells of drink
She doesn't *say*:

You must have done something to make this happen.
You little omnipotent so and so

You have a cough because you're not talking to me
Please talk to me!
It will clear your throat chakra
You're unhappy here.

Maybe it wasna the best use of
500 bucks? Got you that gold rubber duck
From 'The Hollywood Upstairs School of Psychoanalysis'[25]
I used to pass it on Fourteenth Street
I noticed because it was on top of 'Nora Fashions'

Your skin's so thin
Like the bit of old suede
Richard's father
Wrapped the family silver in.

Itheherome extracts books from his woven bag

I carry these.
Heraclitus.
And that prick Francis Bacon.
The father of the scientific method.
Heraclitus—No, that's a snack for later,
Linty coconut ball and rice.
Of course, have some if you like—
Your stomach's been growling all day.
I wouldn't offer if I didn't mean it—

I am reading these two clowns
In preparation
For the next monologue
Attributed to 'The Anchorite'.

She hates Bacon and wants Heraclitus to respect her
Which he never will, obviously.
She speaks with Removed Tongue
I channel her, what of it?
We channel each other, to be precise.

Fuck, do you smell that fucking balloon, again?
It's smelled like balloons all morning
It makes me choke and cry like someone punched me.

Someone *did* punch me, a lot
But I'm smart; I turned out pretty well.
All those goddamned parties

Nothing made any sense.
Rolled up in a rug, they jumped me.
I was the pole in limbo[26]
Rolled up like a fat joint

Still doesn't make sense.
The sound of balloons
Why were people happy?

What was fun about it?
How can that be fun
The sound is worse than the smell

Of balloons
fricative countertenor
Well, sorry but think about it

Words are like that
Think about it hard enough
And you can get pretty darn close
Like stroking a cat the wrong way

> *Itheherome is attaching a little
> chain to the little mosaic.*

The trick,
              the real trick is
Not to.

I'll pop! I'll pop, I tell you!
Bastard balloons
Chickenshit balloons

I think it's my hands?   *Itheherome sniffs*

Yes, that's where it's coming from.
Pee yew. But phew, too.
"It was me all along".
It was the stuff I used to clean the shards
To make this ugly mosaic you can barely
Bring yourself to look at

I found a solvent in a drum
I rolled the drum like a beer keg
Over there, see the big white sink?

It's still there beside it
Will probably be there
For the next thousand years.

I tapped it. Heavy round drops fell
I can feel them now
Near my nipples and near my eyes,

Like that Man Ray photo of tears
I can feel the drops like stuck-in
Half-full ticks all over my body

They fell through the sink and onto the glass
Which came to shine so red
Like a stolen ruby in a heist movie

Voila. Keychain. Are we cool?[27]   *Hands you the keychain*

I hear you and I think that makes a lot of sense.

I hear you and I think that makes a lot of sense.[28]

Well did you know that I believe they faked
The landing on the moon?
I said: I believe they *faked* the moon landing.

You want to go to Riga?
And follow a Jewish Widow?

How did you know I could do that?
You do know me now, a little

That hurts a little

Your wish is my command

1870s.
Nora Iosifovna Chaslovich.

She'll be carting her wares, trinkets and that.
Icons for Catholics, big-eyed tin cats.

Get on my flying carpet, brother mine![29] It's cold this high up
Don't you dare!
Don't you dare
You can hold onto the edges
If you're scared

It is so so dark, close your eyes
The stars are not to be believed

They didn't have streetlights then
And even today I bet they don't here

'Deep into lasting'[30]
Deep
In the countryside

Remember that time in Bearsville
Upstate NY, Woodstock?
You were recording a *wreckchord*
You pulled my hair and pushed me
To my knees by the side of the black road
You were scared of the dark
You were scared
I wasn't really
I like the dark
It makes me almost believe that I exist
When I can't see or be seen

You are afraid of the night.
And the countryside.
Nora knows what she's doing.
We are very safe with her.

Don't worry, dear.

She's been lugging these bits
Of crap back and forth for years
She's too young, twenty-eight
Too young to be widowed

She could have her feet upon an ottoman
In a plush front room
She's had many proposals
From overstuffed twats
Each got a big No Siree Bob.

Luckily her mother understands
Nora loves walking
And she loves her job

And hermeneutics

All she thinks about
Are the stories from the Torah
Playing the plots
Over and over in her head

Interpretation keeps her alive[31]
Her husband was a rabbi
He said she had a great mind
And when he died
Well, no one else would do
Not for a great mind like hers

Listen to the jangling of her pack
She keeps the valuables in the hollow
Of her tall fur hat
(She thought of that!)

Everything's jingling and jangling
Her breath is frozen clouds
Her feet are frozen fish
When she gets to the next town

See it there?
Gaslight, through the paned windows

Here we are. Inside
And straight up to bed

The deaf landlady
Gives her her key and some kefir
Drinking her bottle
On the way upstairs
Do we have to stay?
You have an unprofessional interest in her

Look how you watch her ankles
Each step a little more copper skin shows
Between her skirts and boots

Leave her to sleep,
And her toilet
It's private.

Let's sleep too. I'm tired.

This is the dormitory.
Of course it's empty.
You can choose any bed.
I made them all.

I tell myself about the past.
And how I got here.
It gets me off
To sleep.

The first time Prague's suburbs
Passed my airport bus
I knew I couldn't live out my stupid span
In NYC
Not for you
Not for anybody!

Between sips of wonderful green amber
Becherovka
Downed on Vaclavski Namesti
Under an avenue of limes
Unlike the bloody United States
Where everything's a sign

We argued, remember
You suddenly knew you hated me
(Of course, I had to tell you)

It's just that without a cent
I would have died
You can't deny that that's the case

I used you for your money
But I was a poor gold-digger
Among the worst

Next we went to Moscow on a train
And I was terrified
I was *terrified*

The Moskva was so huge,
So many vodka drunks
Went walking over the bridge with us

By accident we were part of an exodus, a crusade, a mob
There's so much whiteness in a little bottle
Of Stoli

Hungover on a bench in the gardens near the Kremlin
Mothers and their grown-up daughters
In matching patterned dresses
Under a famous oak
Everything is shaded, green and grey
Camouflage day
But the sun is bright
In that way, it reminded me of our home

That was the year before I became a model
I was tired of being stared at
I didn't know what else to do

Remember how you cut my hair
Till I was bald
I was so tired, like now
I was so tired of being blonde
With the Swiss Army nail scissors?
How could you forget that
Of all the things you could forget

Here on the edge of sleep

I feel safe enough to re-approach
Moments of early post-illiteracy
'The Anchorite' will sum up
How Holy Women, not *whores*
      —that was a tragic mistranslation—
Lived in the temple
And men came
Asked if they could come in
The women said,
Fuck yeah

But the men weren't there *all day*
Fucking things up, trying to fuck them
Each other, the kids
Whoever
Having fucking fights
And being idiots

I've never met a wise man.
But because you don't talk
I tell myself you might be.

Your one idea, your one, unoriginal idea
Is that there is a need
For structure

I listen to you
Who else will I listen to?

I am diligent and I am true

I'll copy What is Written
On the board already

Inspired by Nora
I read the Bible
Last night—

You look different this morning
Are you sure you aren't in love?
You've changed your shirt.

I like that it's white
With little fleur-de-lys
Tiny, or maybe they're clubs

I made you a coffee; I make it silty
And these are almond and sugar balls
Wrapped in a mint leaf.
Rosewater makes it adhere
And gives it a feminine taste
Take it or leave it

The Bible's all about how much I suck
Compared to God, compared to Jesus
Compared to men
I threw the fucking thing out of bed

You continued to sleep like a German Shepherd

It hit the wall
And fell chest up
On the floor
Its bosom heaving

It's hard enough with your face
The way it shows every single fucking feeling
Like you were a bell jar
And your eyes the trapped monarch butterfly

Your eyelids are like the wings beating[32]
I can't help imagining
How they would feel to touch
I guess that's beauty
Or maybe it's love?
It's hard enough with your face

Changing to reflect mine
I guess that's beauty
Let's go back to the bazaar
Looks like there's been another bomb

Oh my God, just then
Before you put your glasses on
When you splashed
Your face … just
… Are you a
A dolphin alien[33]
Sent from outer space
To rescue me?

Because, shit
Motherfucker!—
I've never seen
Eyes so far apart

If you can't make sense of it
It doesn't make sense

If it doesn't make sense
You cannot make sense of it

Remember that for later, too
Logic's a kind of epigenetics

Because 'the parts that die
are as important
as the parts that live.'

Remember the other thing?
Learn and suppress at once.
Learn, and *instantly* suppress.

Itheherome sighs

My tiles are intact
The mosaic isn't
I know you didn't like it
But I worked hard on it

Sorry I'm crying
No, my eyeliner won't run
It's tattooed on

I'm just very relieved
No, they aren't magic, my tiles
God, don't be sarcastic

There was a man next door
And he always gave us
Mary Jane Peanut Butter and
Molasses Candies
And my mother said
Just tell him
You are not allowed
To take off your shoes
Then stand in the door
Until Maureen is ready
I don't trust him, he beats his wife
My mother said

I'm very proud of my daughter
I cling to her the way I did
To men sometimes when I was young

The plot worked well
That one we have
Turmoil, desires
Winning near the goal[34]

It worked very well indeed
To make me crazy with desire
Get me out of here, get me out here
I would never scream
God no

Even on my first go
With a Ritalin-snorting friend
The game was rigged:
I was to lose, 'course I knew!

The authors of the Bible weren't all *that* dumb
Like a switch, a woman's love flicks off
After a span of
(googles 'how many breaths do you take in two years')

So they invented Reason
Dressed it up all pretty
Like the cans, newspapers and taffy

Sister.
Sister, don't tell me about refashioning the fucking story
The fucking story is the fucking story
And there is no re-storying

Parmenides' guides, the Sun Goddesses,
As they stand at the gate, know:
Demeter's one true love

Was her daughter

Oh, I can tell you *exactly* when
I knew there was no more : 'about-face'!
I was standing on what looked like
A straight road
On a towpath in the Highlands

Thirty-eight years old,

Then just like that

I couldn't turn my head
My neck was set forever forward
I'd 'broke the back of it'
The trepanning, our rented boat
Three tins of McEwans
(Poured down the new, bloody spout,
The chips of skull
Journeying down my neck and throat
To finally make little incisions
In the walls
Of my small intestine)
Made me the woman I am today

Sorry, I'm overexcited
I want to tell you everything
And I can't make up my mind
Who to pretend I am
I've never had another guest
On the three-legged stool
Or touring with me
My mini-iconography

You weren't sulking when you turned away
It was with innate wisdom
And that blank tarot card
In your solar plexus, glowing

I cannot tell you how much it hurts

> *Itheherome makes a gesture. Holds his*
> *hands one over the other, a foot*
> *between them, then moves them like he*
> *is turning an imaginary globe*

2. The Law[35]

Still here?
You must be
Broke as fuck
I don't pay much

It was someone else's
Life, of course
We always
Forget that
About reincarnation

I spent one lifetime
(an endless afternoon)
On a porch swing
I return only to a single day

Like that blue glass
Single rose
Vase[36] in a poem
I once read about

On this swing
in Falmouth, Mass.
It's raining
I am waiting

For the parade

To pass. Tall
Skinny glass
Of 7-Up

Blue ribbon
On the brim
Of my straw hat

Grown-ups talk.
I can't hear a word
I'm a deaf mute!

I feel safe
As wooden shoes.

Across the lawn
I watch the wind lift
My thin yellow curtain
Through an inch of open

Window. I'd like to watch
The drummers
Their skinny legs
Drums strapped
The sticks moving
So so fast!

But they never come.
Someone elbows me to eat
What's being passed around
I'm given a look, but
I feel good empty.

Maybe that's why
My favourite sense
Is sound, because:
"Once in New England..."

I was a deaf child
Well looked after
Loved, safe
Missing one thing
Like it was everything

*

Amor Fati
Means
Love your fate.
Louise Glück
Sent me a ring

She worried and worried
That it would not arrive
She paid the insurance
She sent it and worried

She could have been my mother
I wish she had been my mother

The ring will arrive.
Rest easy, dear Louise.
I said, and it did.

Louise *chose* for me
A ring her sister, the jeweller
Therez made
And it said AMOR FATI

Black courier font
Inlaid in gold vermeil.

Heavy letters
That go deep

The thick ring
Always twists to:

FAT

Makes my finger look it
And check it, it's a thin finger

He sticks up his left ring finger
onto which the ring is squished
and all you can read
is the word FAT

Louise and her sister Tereze

Like a Balthus painting
Two fighting girls
Their glabrous brows alight

In a dim living room
Plastic slip-covers, 50s sitting room

My father was Louise's ideal
He was beautiful

He was a star philosophy student
He was beautiful

She was a recovering anorexic
With an axe to grind

A nice Jewish boy
Joseph, that was my father's name.

Louise and Tereze's dad and his brother
Invented the X-Acto blade

My father's father
Was the editor-in-chief

Of the women's magazine *Redbook*
And his mother

Was the chief administrator
Of a big mental hospital

Struck gold with the X-Acto
The Glück brothers did

A nice Jewish boy and a few dollars
Will get you on the IRT
But a jowly middle aged junkie on a skateboard
Can take you exactly—

On the weekends

I watched my father
Slice his feet, repeatedly.
(How can you not know what
An X-Acto blade is!
A metal version
Of a plastic sceptre
Wielded by
A Lego castle guard)
In his work he used
Boxes of X-Acto blades.
So many uses.
It splices. It makes what you read.[37]
He sat on his linty swivel chair
In front of the elephant-sized
Typesetting machine
A dark daisy with a fluffy Jewfro

His trusty apparatus, cop car blue
All around him in a circle on the floor
The discarded wands of
X-Acto blades, like stems
Thrown by a deranged
Little girl in a field of poppies
Caught up in her OCD
Three hours of *he loves me, he loves me not*
He screamed and laughed at once
 'Drat! Drat!' he laughed and cried
The blood left brown rainbows
On the painted white floorboards

The X-Acto blade wore many cutting hats
Aside from aiding in the production of club invites
Which was his regular job
After he burned his PhD[38]
The X-Acto blades loosed chunks of cocaine
From impacted rubber fingertips
Smuggled by way of South America
In the swallowed knotted fingers
Of dismembered rubber gloves

That whole thing was impacted

It was impossible to write and you can tell

Real life is like that, mine at least

You try to write it like it is
And everything 'crumbles back into the moat'[39]
Every goddamned detail of what really happened
Is so relentlessly unlikely
Look close, and you will see the same applies to you

(Remember that painting?
The *Nostalgia of the Infinite*,[40]
The big rubber glove by the building?
De Chirico?
You must. Me and you
Used to walk downtown to MOMA
The sidewalks were so hot
I wore a tank top[41] and no bra
And my Jehovah sandals.
I think that summer you were wearing
A Crazy Eddie baseball cap
Once there we'd stare and stare
And you would sometimes take my hand
Then remember who I was
And quickly
Let go)

Someone had
Shat out these fingers.
My dad explained,
Jovially,
His eyes tearing
Over the chemicals

From the typesetting fixer
He was using to clean his own blood
From the floor and his foot
Isn't that disgusting? I'd say
And he'd say
Not really.

Typesetter: a profession that died
Its letters replaced
By a non-aesthetic.
Art is in the middle of sign and symbol

I hate everyone

It's no coincidence we meet again

I don't think so

Allow me to remind you how I
Could have died
I think that's why
Spirits can see me
At the National Portrait Gallery
For example

Did you know you can moan your way

                              back to consciousness?

13 days old. Oregon, Wisconsin:
I wanted to leave now
Day 13, out of the muted
Stoned womb
Into the Dionysion world
Too smokey
Too sunny
Too noisy
My mother—too blank
She took me for a cat or dog
My brother wanted to kill me
I could taste the DDT that sprayed
From the plane over the corn fields
Behind our house
Yeah, the placenta had split.
Gorgeous rented costume, gone.
So I, a quick study,
'Initiated my own abandonment'
Endeavoured to catch
My death—whooping cough

I regret them saving me in that box,
Fucking technological advances of the
Early 70s. I regret my rescue
Maybe that's why I hate stories

　　　　　Do I have a nice mouth?
　　　　　　　Because you're *always* looking at it.
　　　　　　　　Just my tongue in there, buddy.
　　　　　I know it darts around a lot

I don't blame you for anything   that's part of our problem
You make total sense   I hear you and I think

It's the *soundproofing*
On the walls in that room
Above the mosque
Don't ask me why
It bothers my tongue
Or why the last tenant put
That stuff up

*

Souls drooping heavy

Still full of water

Lamp posts
Avenues of limes

Alleged transcriptions of symbolism
Drawn from frayed little picture cards

'The salt shaker symbolises treason'[42]
I guess I could *try* to see

These dead armies as copses
Colour as black and white

Shrouds as flags or better, bunting
This backwater as the cure
And that giant moss coated chandelier?[43]
On its long jute rope
Like a B-movie radioactive tarantula
In the middle of the Champs-Elysees
What the hell could that be—
Shutting down and opening up
Like a sea anemone or magic shop
Delicately dropped from the puppeteer's fingers

*

What shite
I stopped right there
When I was fifteen

I write like this now
I see colour, the dead and death

I am sorry for how I've mistreated you
It's not your fault.
It's mine.

It is Written: it is the law.

Another Sociopath

My first mother-in-law
'Hated me at first' as she put it
Truth is she never stopped
I grew to love her in spite of that
And that taught me a lot
It's weird loving someone
Who hates you. And it's also weird
Having someone say they love you
When they hate you. Richard?
Your mum, when she was dying
Called me to her hospital bed
Brought into her lovely study
And placed where her desk had been
She faced the garden
She called me to her
Amidst my daughter's
13th birthday
Which, considering,
Was fairly upbeat
And Alison Jolly, primatologist
Asked me if she could have a sip
Of my gin and tonic
It broke my heart to tell her
It was soda water.
I'd sobered up. Years before.
She hadn't noticed.
She never noticed me
She thought I was a completely different person
Than who I am, because of the face
And the Dalek delivery

If she had only listened
To my words
Primatology might have been
A different science.
Then she told me
About how the village floods
The exact order in which
The Winterbourne
And its streamlets burst
Which streets and roads
The water follows
She began to call herself the flood
To refer to the water as I.
No one else heard this
I wondered
If it was because
She knew hallucinations
Don't scare me
Because my father was Joseph
Or maybe she knew
I'd seen him die too
For all his counter-culture posturing
Her end was more interesting
That's pain meds for ya.
Because he said,
"Tell maw and paw I love them" or
Some trite shite
And Alison Jolly, the famous primatologist
And my ex-mother-in-law

Who always hated me
And loved Desmond Morris
Told me on her death bed
That the river Ouse[44]
Finally had won from her
Her point of view.

*

My real life?
You were there.
A beat-up
Nike shoebox
Diorama
Dirty Plasticine in unknowable shapes
Draw a square on the inside with a magic marker
Then the negative space, its cardboard-colour is fine
(Don't worry about that level of detail)
For the courtyard wall
The whole place faces that wall

With this e-cig
Be my dolly grip
Stand back a foot
Exhale
Marijuana scented
Vapour

And the whole time
Bang pots and pans
Bang them and bang them
Bang the shit out of them
And scream over them:

Don't call me a woman   *The Love Boat*

Don't call me a little girl   *Fantasy Island*

Don't call me alive   *Three's Company*

Don't call me dead   *The Facts of Life*

In two dreams I can't forget
I'm with two brothers
In one we are all in the front seat

            It's snowing on the bridge
                        Driving over a long bridge, at night
                Spoke after spoke, glows
                        And suspends us, as we
                Approach
        Then falls behind, and I can see the lights
Arching away

Over the curve of the earth and a strong river
In the rear view mirror[45]

In the other dream
We are all downtown
In a city I don't know
But know in the dream

In both dreams
I'm 'all bundled up'
Hat, gloves, scarf, coat.

When I wake up I
Hold my kimono sleeve
Over my mouth[46]
As I respectfully throw the book
I'm sleeping with aside
Struck by the beginning
Of *Madame Bovary*
Of course, to start with Charles!

Look, it hurts
To take up God's calling
Because you think it is His
But God, as my daughter said
May not be omnipotent

To which I replied that Narrative was
A technological innovation
Hastily drawn up
To coincide
With the unveiling
Of that glorified to-do list
The Bible

At any rate...
Stories
From the age of four,
Floored me

Poorly laid, cheap lino
Ya'll got the sexist
Australian handyman
On the cheap—but Christ,
at what price?

Tawdry, false, chemical, sticky.
And so patently untrue.

> *With silver buttons buttons*
> *buttons all down her back back back*
> *Miss Mary Mack Mack Mack*
> *all dressed in black black black*

She's on a swing

After the Greasy Spoon
In a pink bathroom
Down a long red carpeted hall
Green dish soap used as shampoo

Eight year-old Maureen,
Whose father we believe beats her mother
Will administer the proceedings
Because my mother is
Beginning to suspect that I may be human
And has raised her palm,
Dragged on her jay, and shut
The bathroom door.
My eyes burned so much
I wanted to scratch them out

In 1974 in Chicago, Illinois

My father puts the light of a firefly
On the turning record *Help*
And I jump up and down
As the metal coils
Make crowbar noises
From inside the bed

When I was younger, so much younger than today
I never needed anybody's help in any way

A two-year-old
Nostalgic for someone else's
Naïveté

Stevie stole my skyscraper tulip
He eyed me from outside the fence
I wondered if I should let him in
I knew that he would rip it up
I knew because I was so young
I could still show myself the future
But I let the little shit in anyway
I wanted to show it to him
I wanted to. I wanted to.
Then he ripped it up
And I chased him through the whole
White trash neighbourhood
screaming and crying.
"Give me back
my fucking tulip
You little shit!"

I was three. We had to move
From Chicago to NYC.
You can't stay with those crazy
hick assholes
Also my father drove my mother
Round the bend
She felt even when
He didn't say a word
'He was criticising her.'

A liminal space
Amtrack / Travel
Destroys
Both places
Origin and destination.
Chicago and New York
In the train carriage
I wondered if
It was ok to eat
Sleep or pee?
We had berths
But walking through the cars
Of the passengers
Who couldn't afford beds

Made me wish
That I was dead

I'd have a thousand miles
Between me and everyone
Alive or dead

Bunched together like that,
People I meet practically disappear
Bunched like that, their heads flopping
Like picked wildflowers the instant
You pull 'em up.

Reminds me of a drooping
Bunch of clown flowers
I once daydreamed
You brought me

You brought them to me at my door
Handed them to me as I opened it
You looked at the ground
Walking the stoned path
Through the front garden
I am never going to have

It's ok—we can't all get the prize
I've got a little cash, and I can pay

A word is a dummy
A stand-in,
A bitter understudy
Who wins because he cheats

I realise it might have been
Offensive what I said about symbolism
And it was only in response
To some damn fool
Who was insisting on the Primacy
Of Symbolic Gestures
On Facebook, of all places

Me and the house become one
I'd gladly be rising damp—gladly
To be at home with you

Drinking a tall 7-Up

Cross-legged in the centre
On an old trampoline
Fair Edina
Fine morning
In the overgrown
Tenement gardens
Pea flowers
Usurping and humping a fuchsia
The size of a van

Why I left Dundee?
You caught somma my crazy,
Big fella?
Not as easy as it looks in here
          Is it? Eh no dad, is it?
Why are you
Even asking that
What do you care?

          Savouring the encouragement, Itheherome lies down
          on her back and stares at the stars, her fingers
          threaded through her long blonde hair. Her tanned
          knees fall open like a hardback book

Man, the scorn
Of that city is—

Shit …

I'd been writing *The Geographic*,
The novel I mentioned
I chose not to finish it—choice exists—
It was set in a top flat
At the bottom of Infirmary Brae

Solange Cogshell's flat overlooked
You did ask!—
The Ladywell Roundabout[47]
Also called simply a 'circle'

She was to have ended there
'Fished up'
As Jean Rhys said, in her dour
Incontestable way

After many misadventures
Among them having her life story
Told by an incompetent, rebellious
But ultimately lovable
Omniscient Narrator
(The fossil I mentioned)

And was going to die there, I was pretty sure

So it started with her asleep
Circled back
à la *Goodfellas*
We started three-quarters in

The best structure, for these days
In my humble opinion
Covers a multitude of sins

But we had sold up
And the building burned

He wanted to stay in Dundee forever

He said, och aye it's crap
But it's cheap and hame
And the folk are
Dead nice

On even the most Stupid Holidays
St Patrick's and St. Valentine's, say
Relevant Helium Balloons
Appeared in the peeling and melting
Bay window, leered down at the brae
It will have had
One of those
Electric cookers
With four plates
Coated with white
Metal curds
From decades
Of splattered mince juice
Dundee's vengeful hand
Ripped the whole top flat

Aff the tenement
This was a month or so before I left
I was walking
Thinking of Solange
Looked up to her flat
And fucked if it wasn't torn away
Like the barn at the beginning
Of *The Wizard of Oz*

Our new place already bought
Dundee felled the yew
In the Howff
Where a vital love scene was meant
To erupt
Between a Dr. and a patient
I hadn't written it yet
But lemme tell you it was
Keeping me going.

The City of Discovery
Scuppered my third novel.

I may not believe in symbols
But I sure as shit believe in signs[48]

So you can sit there
(Which is as it should be)
On your three-legged chair.
I squat, as you'll have noticed
I haven't sat in a chair
In years: it fucks your back

Yes back to me, back to Dundee—
The supporting beams remained
Like the sides of a beeswax candle
Did she die? Solange? In a fire?

A melding of the
Disempowered
Omniscient Narrator
And the disenfranchised
Character

I hadn't figured out
Exactly how

It ends

During that time in Dundee

> *It was said I was a this*
> *It was said I was a that*
> *It was said it wasn't fair*
> *Except with tit for tat*
>
> *Not a penny, year in year out.*
> *She didn't earn a penny*
> *Not a penny*

It was my best novel, so far

But really,
Come on
What's the point?
A house of playing cards
Outmoded parlour game
Sentimental pastime
That sits in the box
With a dumb retro design
Of some arsehole white family
Around a table
It's all about the box
That's it in a box
While aw cunt and sundry
They binge-watch TV
While the top flat burns

Little bit of bread and no cheese
Little bit of bread and nae cheese
Not a penny, year in and year out
Not a fucking penny, year in and year oot

3. The Lock[49]

for Craig Raine

Just kidding
Fuck you, Craig Raine

Have I told you lately
How much you fucking suck
To quote Kurt Cobain,[50]
Craig Raine

Did I tell you about the time
We went to Robin Hood, Maine,

Craig Raine?

Ken yer faither
Fatty Patty
The Tudor Tatty!
And I also have
Your back.
Do you
Have mine?
Aye, I ken ye dinna

Eh no dad?
Nut!
Eh dad, is it?
Is it sut!

But ye can
Tak a photie
Of yersel
As a lass
And the app
Makes ye
Look like a lass
It's funny,
I was pure
Creasin up
Eh no dad?
Is it?!?!
See the Tay bridge dad?
We are going over it now

Aye son

The sun on the sparkly Tay
Like a trillion million silver fishes' scales[51]
A million silver arrowheads

From the Hudson to the Tay, and back again!

The perforated
Leather seats
No air-conditioning
Grandpa's old Datsun

1980

On the highway
Queuing at the tolls
'Crossing state lines'
Connecticut snakes into NY

I wasn't afraid
Of being born,
Why should I
Be afraid of dying?

My mother had to work very hard
To make me afraid of death

She also worked very hard at
The Brew Burger
When we moved to NYC
From Chicago

There were cockroaches
In the relish

My front tooth
The naked yacht
The deserted island

All the adults were naked
And they were all men
You couldn't turn but for to see
A hairy ass crack
A dick hanging long
And for some reason
Pulled up socks and knees

> *If not for the courage of the fearless crew,*
> *the Minnow would be lost,*
> *the Minnow would be lost.*[52]

The grown-ups fucking
In the maple loft

Getting stuck
At low tide
My brother and I
In the inlet

We needed pried
Our boots left there
In the mud without us
Overnight

I loved that

Though it was my first tooth
I was not allowed up
To the cherry
Loft bed
Where my mom

Fucked her male host's
Boyfriend
I stood at the foot
Of the ladder
And called
"My tooth came out!"

Someone had French braided my hair
The dinner would be formal
We'd sit at the long table
I would wear ribbons and a dress

But the meal was a washout
Everyone got drunk before they cooked
The corn on the cob was forgotten
For some reason I want to tell you:
How much I wanted to eat it because
Some girl on a TV show
Couldn't eat hers, with her tooth missing
I wanted to see whether I could.

In the mirror
I disliked the braids
Thin as mouse tails
Looked like bulging veins
My under-eyes a rheumy grey

And that split where my forehead fused wrong

"That is great!"
The Dutchman said

Since my mom arrived
They decided Bhagwan[53]
Wasn't all that after all!
They did drink whiskey after all!

'She brought the city with her.'[54]

"Keep it and the Tooth Fairy
May come!"
The Dutchman said

His blonde moustache
His red face

He made us rake the lawn
He said
We needed stability and order
You don't remember?
Truth be told
It helped

With my three dollars
I bought a stuffed ape

My mother laughed and laughed
She nodded her small head
Knowingly
Her legs spread wide
She stood like a man

'Now when the next tooth goes
We won't be able to understand
A word you say.'[55]

On the way home
My brother
Pulled single hairs
From my head
While singing
'100 Bottles of Beer'

The Datsun died
And the dog, almost
Of thirst
Hard to believe that we
Survived by
Walking beneath
The CT, NY tolls
Metal bridges
Underground
This is no dream!

This is really happening!⁵⁶
We waited at an IHOP
But couldn't afford anything
There was a thunderstorm
Then it was less hot

Some things are so straightforward

And my father
Drove to meet us
From his loft on Lafayette
He hardly dropped everything
My mother said
Eating strawberry syrup
Off the back of her spoon
Because we had been waiting three
Hours with no money
Only enough for her coffee
And my dad
'Had clearly had time
to wash his hair'

(In later years I cut his hair
And he never did. Wash.
Did you know junkies
Are self-cleaning?
They never ever
Feel dirty.
They never ever
Feel guilty. They so very rarely

Have to piss or shit.
So all the good emotions
Get stuck in, like honey.
It's sublime, in some ways
Try it sometime.)

Is it my turn?
No!
I can't believe it.
I wasn't lying when I said
I had no hope.
You looked sad,
Well—

OMG!
Shout out to God![57]
I'm so happy
Smiling like
Miss America

High heels and a bathing suit
With that mad baton,
Sceptre, is it?
Or is it a bouquet?
Anyway, please,

Bury my heart
On Mechanic Street
In Provincetown, Massachusetts
Where we lived that winter
When Frances was a baby

My severed fingers
Individually place
Between the tracks
Of the subway

At 72 Street and Broadway
Like piano keys
I stood on that platform
Many a hungover morn

Please drive both eyeballs
On the golf course
In St. Andrews
At the Cathedral near that funny
Little archway in the corner

I used to pretend we were stuck
When Frances was in her pram
She loved that joke
I twitched her carriage madly

My liver feed to my dogs
Caprica 6 and Yentl
But don't overcook it
Pink in the middle

(Have you met the drunk
Spaniard with...)

Proceed to the breakwater
Where
The pacing ghost
Of the postmaster's wife walks

(… the white pug
Named Gordito?)

Now, progress to the dunes where
Rolled up bodies
In blankets left by a serial killer
        (I was the pole in limbo)
Who called it his marijuana garden

Women's bodies in bowling alleys

It's impossible to say just what I mean[58]
But I think Richard will remember, ask him
What we were like.
What *were* we like!

Waiting for the subway
Hot like a sauna
And almost as nice
I'm a hydroponic houseplant
Light through the grates
Down there
All human passion high above[59]
You couldn't see anyone's better life

Forever panting and forever young[60]
Getting and spending.[61]

The beaches' coasts are infinite not because
They're fractal, asshole
But because they belong to dead children
Their little fingernails are the scum of waves
Sunrise and sunset look exactly the same
Sunrise and sunset are *almost exactly the same*

Now that I'm dead will you listen to me?
My little girl's fingers are the tide dragging
Along the West Sands
I'll be quite far along
Closer to Tentsmuir
Than St. Andrews
The moon and the sun's ratio of fit
Is a coincidence
But coincidence
Is a very very
False word

Do you like pearls?
Do you know how they make them?
Incisions.
I meant to take you so many places
To where Frank O'Hara got hit
On Fire island
To where Hart Crane jumped
Off the George Washington Bridge
I'm really sorry

You only got the widow

When my mouth sealed shut
I realised I looked exactly like
That spirit guide
A YouTube guy
Conjured in me
Yeah, I was doing
A YouTube video
To find your spirit guide
On my phone.
I get lonely like everyone else
Sometimes I imagine
My mouth is full of pearls
And shells and skin, I'm drowned
Sand all around me
Underwater
And I'm changing
Into the world again

What's the thetic, Julia Kristeva?
I always loved the name Julia

Half of what I say is meaningless
But I say it just to reach you, Julia
Julia[62]

I named my cheap anglepoise lamp
Julia, because it was new
I didn't get new things
How the metallic green paint gleamed!
It looked so modern
With its bendy plastic arm
Broke within a week

I kept her anyway

Over in the corner
By the big iron radiator
She's probably still there
Will probably be there
For a thousand years[63]

My mother's there

My spirit guide was me as a kid
Not what I was led to expect
I wanted an angel like the Good Witch

Some pretty lady in a bubble[64]
No joy—I had a fish body
No legs to speak of, more of a wheel
A truncated spiral
Of rotting scales

My face was mummy-covered
With mouldy jute
My hair was the same

My dead gran from rural Maine talks to me
"You always look lovely dear
You're a great beauty
I'd brush my hair
If I were you
Amazing that you are still blonde
At 45."

I'm always gonna have it
Mine will be a skull
With blonde hair
One of those mummies you see
On the cover of a science magazine
Those poor souls who haven't
Felt 'the pleasures of decomposition'
Truth is, I'm starting to look like one already
It's the fake tan, and I'm too skinny

'Put your oxygen mask on first'?
Yeah you told me
Like twenty fucking times
That's the stupidest metaphor
I've ever heard
And I've 'followed a few'
Come on, don't walk away

You can't get anywhere from here
That's why they call it the desert
That's *why* we're here

Seriously though,
You can't talk, kiss,
And you're going down, to boot?

What a waste of fucking love this all is
What a waste of fucking love

See these? These marionette slits
At the corners of my jute mouth?
Like Heath Ledger in *The Dark Knight*?

> *Itheherome touches his lips,*
> *imitates the dead actor,*
> *not well:*

"Wanna know how I got these?"

A little bit of truth ripped them
May have happened no matter what
Or maybe it's circumstances

When you said that about the tree
With three trunks
The one I'd met around the time
I first met you

I leaned way back into its arms

She leans back

A move I innocently demonstrated
In your consulting room

Then you said I'd only let someone hold me
When no one was looking.

It made my skin crack open
Nice hack, that's the turtle's back
You lying sap

A student with a severed hand tattoo

It was fenced off the next time
I went to visit the tree

A young man had been found
In the loch where the tree stood
Behind police tape

A student with a severed hand tattoo
Drowned drunk,
Drunk, drowned

I looked at my willow
Her three roots stuck in the mud
Wishing I could lie in her arms

But then she bellowed from afar:

Itheherome, get the fuck outta here
Itheherome, yes he has a huge cock,
Happy?

Fucking lewd tree with a Long Island accent
I never thought about *that*
Well, except maybe in terms of
How it might have affected you…

No, *I* wondered what terms of endearment we'd use.
None seemed right, baby
Easy money, baby

Walking away

Walking away from you, the tree

The dead body with the severed hand tattoo

Onwards!

To the Union Canal
Its high water

Screw that Tourette's-ass tree

I'll follow the dribble of the green Union Canal
Where Caitrin told me
There was once a whorehouse
Called Fingertips

Screw that fucking Tourette's-ass tree

I can see the Pentlands
Two stripes on the ski slopes
Like a thick zipper on a kid's coat
A bouncy boatless dock
(*Why'd you say that?*
What you getting at?)
On the boatless dock

The air catches on the surface of the water
Pointy trinkets in the sun,
They bought Manhattan for—how many dollars?
Twenty-four. Correct.
Hung in memory on a fence or lamppost
Tied in memory of some colossal human tragedy
Jangling and jangling wryly in the dry breeze

Walking away from you
Walking away from the tree
From the dead body with its
Corny-ass severed hand tattoo

I don't need a mask
They fixed me
I breathe any old air
Breathe water too

th: (the voiceless dental fricative)

When my mother mentioned
She would cark it
In no very long
I shoogled the broken drawer in the heavy chest
Found zilch
It wasna hate
It was a total absence
Which made *me* want to die
I wonder if Virginia Woolf chose
The rocks she stuffed her pockets with with care
I would. I have one here—
I call him
The Omniscient Narrator.
He is cursed with a human mouth, eyes,
Nose and chin. You've met him.

All my life I've been trying to not tell the truth and not to lie.
I knew speaking the truth would make me ugly but lying was
out of the question. Every sentence hurts to compose, *but it
can be done.*

'Well I guess that's one way to finally find out the difference
between a concussion and a contusion.' If you are conscious
and puking you're contused.

Little bit of bread and no cheese
Not a penny year in year out
She didn't earn a penny
Not a penny! Year after year

Once I enrolled in a prep course
For the test for law school
No shit, and the first day
In a taxi down Broadway
I was all, fuck this for a game of soldiers
Look at all the traffic lights
Swinging triptychs
A ruby, an emerald, and a yellow citrine
Shoved in a cube of dull ochre plasticine.
Look at the river
Giant fulfilling snake

The lumps in you
Swelling up and down
Moving downtown
Bodies or garbage bags
Beside empty tugs
Plowing the Hudson
Lights reflecting

My brother has a parrot
My brother has a parent
A parrot named Paco
And the parent is an asshole

Painstaking?
That's what you'd call it, Heraclitus?
You do know your name has the word 'clit' in it?
And mine has the word 'ass' in it
I told you we'd be friends, in the end

I've stepped in the same Hudson River
So many thousands of times

I hit myself in the face
In front of Richard
And he didn't react
This was about a week ago

Warm and full of love
But 'capable of discernment'
Cold and detached
Was the cat[65]

Sometimes the rose gold barrette
Lying on the table in the sun
And the sound of the fat black fly
And the cars in the road

In front of my old house
These sounds

My dogs stomping
Into the shade under the bed
The babies screaming

In the triangle of park out the window

Someone moving kegs into

The Links pub
Under me

Sorry
I forgot I was here
'Property is theft'
That's what I keep
Forgetting to say

Suddenly I can hear; I'm not deaf anymore
In the Grange cemetery
Trinket tree, a silver birch,
A marching band
Militaristic drummers

"These things happen."

Anjali said,
As I held her hand
In St Leonard's
Near Arthur's Seat
She's afraid of heights plus mud (slippage)
She said,

"My friend's mother
Told me, you don't know what bad fairy
Or local equivalent
Is listening
So shush
With the cruel things
You say about yourself.
Who are you to judge."

Anjali told me she drank salt water
Brought to the banks of the Ganga
In her yoga training
But didn't puke it up
Like she was supposed to

I believe that was the day I finally figured out what lyricism is.

After our walk she dragged me into a chapeau shop[66]
Every hat looked good on her

In every line in every poem
That you ever wrote
You're telling me

Something about yourself
That you think I want to hear
So if you're a hero or a drone
A drunk or a dumbass

You've rigged the angle of the stage
And are slipping closer
Seemingly
Unintentionally

Lyricism
Couldn't be
Less
Natural

To me at least.

Besides,

There's only
So much
A girl
Can take

Fucksake

Three Endings

1.

When he's at home?
I don't know
Probably disappears
When he's supposed to be
In the hall between rooms

Only to like
Rematerialise in the bog
Taking thon
Macho midnight poet's pish[67]

The thetic's there
Eh Julia?
Nice one?
Yer a funny lass.
Good one.

I'm in the sunny cemetery
Standing under a copper beech tree
That makes that noise
Stiff skirts and tin cats, Nora's here

I can see now that the red tulip
Was a phallus, metaphorically—
I'm kidding
It was a beautiful flower
The safety of its tubular
I'll stop there

Why not trace your
Mary Jane toe in
The pinkish gravel

Of the leaf-fringed[68] graveyard
Observing the simultaneous trajectories
Of (count 'em) thirteen ants
As you did at four years-old
When you studied everything small
Years spent only observing
You looked and looked
Look at that
Look at that teeny wee thing, how it moves
Keep looking, learn, and do not
Do not talk until
You know what
You're saying

The first self is small and in proportion to the World
(I know shrinks think the opposite—
But I for one luxuriated in my puniness)
Then it swells to a problematic size
Until it begins to Fall again

Warmth and intensity
No one told me were physical

Pulled like single hairs from my scalp[69]
Give what I had to someone else, then

To redistribute

Nora Campbell, a twenty-three-year-old
In the graveyard
'The Shadows Flee away.'

I used to be a model, can you tell?
I know it makes you mad
When I mention it
Because you believe your impression of me
Belongs solely to you

And because I'm I the hero me now

Well, tough titty
As we said in the 70s

> *Once and for all the curse*
> *Of proud Itheherome bellows*
> *Thru the cobbled streets*
> *Of Edinburgh*

> *You Mary Poppins, motherfucker!*
> *Sent from Queens or wherethefuckever!*
> *To oversee a well-judged*
> *Phallic interlude*

> *What has your ease taught you,*
> *Hindenburg?*
> *Except that yet again*
> *My pain is my own fault*
> *For what you saw as a lack*

Where I know there's a door

Scottish Green Marble, remember you asked?
Scottish Green Marble. That's my favourite stone.
Looks like snot, but I love it. Mucous rock.[70]
I like opals too, but everyone knows they
Balance your karma. To be avoided.

>   That Perspex bed stroke box
>   Solitary igloo block for a baby

I don't like other folk beside me in my bed
I hear the drumming of my own heart in my head

And finally one more thing The Sun Goddesses said
At the chain link fence to the afterlife (Chicago):

'Everything in the whole world is conscious
That's obvious, but listen:
For a small eternal debt
I'll teach you how to trick humans
Into forgetting'

And now
Before a live audience
At the King's Theatre
In my sheer stockings
>   (The ladder has started, very high,
>   up the thigh, no one knows)

Asking about an old man's long-dead father
And his very long book, light as a cloud however
I know I shouldn't talk

But, consider this: how else could I allow myself
To speak so freely?

I take my single, barely credible, bow

2.

The Last Sociopath

Well well well
A wretched dénouement
Who would have guessed?
In this narrativeless hinterland
Hello fucking tree
We meet again.
Three prongs of earthly desire
Three roots
Have you for an open—

Down you go
Bog willow
This axe chops
The horny seat

Uh oh, I'm not alone lochside

Straw woman at noon o'clock
Feeding Warburtons
To the Eider ducks
Doesn't she know
It gums them up

She eyes me carefully
Raises her voice
                'almost imperceptibly'
But so that I will hear:
She's the mum
Knows exactly how,
To talk down to
Her little son

Hey Lady
Condescension's not the sign
Of a job well done!

3.

            The arms of the jam-encrusted
            Princess Leah action figure
            Are doing Tai Chi
            Cloud Hands, then reverse
            She's a windmill
            Hands, Winnicott, hands![71]

There's no time, man!
After the deluxe burger at the Greasy Spoon
The nice lady gave me a Yoohoo
And she held my hand
And the thickening sun oozéd down
Nearly killing the baby leaves
In and between the tiers
Of the tall sycamores
Like the rising circles at the King's Theatre
And she took me to the playground
I felt so loved, even by
The hot metal swings
That burned my bare thighs
Nothing beats that, Chicago
It was the happiest I'd ever been
Then on the way back to my dad
My whole hand got locked
In the trunk of her Mustang
With the keys!
No kidding!
And a crowd gathered
And they all said:
What a brave little girl!
What an incredibly brave little girl!

Each time I am rejected
I become
                    more and more myself,

This Creature

Black Lagooness
Mothra
Frankenstein
And Jesus

And guess what, asshole?
The next time we meet
In the next life,
I'm going to do
The same exact thing to you.
Again and again and again.
Life after life after life.
I was made a broken record
For your ears only
Nightmare, eh? Eh no dad, is it?
I'm going to be me, and me
And me, and me again
Until you give me
What I want

Your surrender will feel—
Well, I don't know how you feel
About surrender—but if I may,
The healthy posture would be
Something like this:

I fought Itheherome
She kicked my fucking ass
Now I will hold her
In my ochre arms

And we will side by side
Approach the garden path
Its borders lined
With white porcelain, *Grolsch* beer bottle tops
And costly, Hélène Cixous basalt rocks,
From the margins
Edible orange chrysanthemums
Look up to red geraniums
In cracked pots
Humming with bees[72]

Then finally,
The rain stops

Nora has put all this
In the ground
With those dinky
Book spine wrists
For three years
Wound in the dirt
She explained,
How her fingers feel

I'll hear what she has always said
My throat will knot
I'll nod my head
My heart will overflow

And that will break the spell
Cast fifteen thousand years ago

I'll love her
        For the Creature that she is
And see she's always been

                    my girl at the gates.

1   Gilligan was a goofy character in the ensemble sitcom, *Gilligan's Island*, which was made in the late 60s but was in syndication when I was a kid. It's about a tour group who go out on a yacht in a storm and get marooned.

2   Allusion to that stupid Paul Muldoon poem, 'The Loaf'

3   Allusion to the wonderful W.S. Graham poem, Loch Thom.

4   'Think', the Aretha Franklin song.

5   'The Rime of the Ancient Mariner'

6   The promise made at the start of game shows.

7   My friend Yona used to translate an Italian, and maybe Romanesco, idiom into English thusly: he has an ass for a face.

8   This is not anti-Semitic. I'm half Ashkenazi Jew and (while we are here) deeply grateful for the Jewish tradition of questioning I was raised with; it taught me to think. The vision of this nasty man, I came to realise, was an embodiment of the Ashkenazi cancer gene (BRCA mutation). It makes you more likely to get ovarian, prostate, breast and (probably) colon cancer. I have always had visions of strangers, as detailed and individual as real people. They represent various ailments and threats, including Covid 19; who was a drunk, blonde and stupid teenage boy, the kind who would drug your drink.

9   Please note this garden path and its recurrence later.

10   Double allusion to Ted Berrigan and William Carlos
      Williams.

11   'America', Allen Ginsberg

12   *All in the Family*, you may be familiar with the American
      sitcom about the irascible bigot with a heart of gold—I
      know; it was based on a British sitcom I've never seen
      but am told I should mention as this book is being
      published in Britain: *'Til Death Us Do Part*.

13   This construction is from something but I can't remem-
      ber what.

14   Many years ago I listened to the Bob Dylan song
      'Hurricane' a lot, and in it he sings, 'in the hot NJ night'.

15   'The Love Song of J. Alfred Prufrock', T.S. Eliot

16   *Paradise Lost*. Satan loves chiasmus, the banal fuck.

17   To clear up any confusion Madame Bildungsroman was
      born as slur for the character of the Omniscient Narrator
      in my unfinished third novel the Geographic. In it, this
      narrator was widely reviled by a circle of non-human
      narrators (of which they were one) and was often insul-
      ted, called things like Cuntry Doctor. Slowly this feck-
      less nonsoul had their powers revoked, and struggled to

tell the tale with no omniscience, no memory; eventually they could neither hear nor see, but being committed and having only one purpose they continued to tell the story as best they could until the bitter end. It's a sad story. For various reasons I could not find the heart to finish the novel so I started writing a blog, called *Madame Bildungsroman's Optimistic Worldview*. I had no followers until Airea Dee Matthews started reblogging me. Needless to say, we became fast friends. I continued to write the blog to amuse her, mostly. And Madame B became a character within it, a grumpy, demanding, paper mache effigy who dies at the end. And if you could follow that—you're in the right place!

18   Aka the Devonian, a geologic period.

19   My father had a line in a poem that was a little like this, 'storming up stairs that haven't existed in forty years', I think it was. I can't be bothered taking his little book down off the shelf.

20   She means 'disentangled' but she is thinking of how painful 'detangling' her thread-like hairs were, after baths, when he was a little girl.

21   Everything I know about Parmenides and the Sun Goddesses I learned from Peter Kingsley. A book called *Reality*, with large type and questionable credentials; it was recommended to me by Barbara Barg. God rest her.

22   *Rosemary's Baby*

23   'The Love Song of J. Alfred Prufrock'

24   A bunch of rocks set up to prevent water eroding land, often very interesting to look at. Or maybe that's just me.

25   cf. Dr. Nick's School of Upstairs Medicine on *The Simpsons*.

26   I am told here in the UK we say limbo pole and that no one will get pole in limbo.

27   *Tropic Thunder*

28   My shrink.

29   Unfortunately this is from the TV show *Sherlock*. I took it out but kept hearing it. So I put it back.

30   *I Ching*. I have never understood what it means.

31   I'm better at the dialectic: ask me questions. No. You refuse. You are afraid. That's why I've been known to revert to my true self. I was born in Madison, Wisconsin, in 1972, a polyphonic novel trapped in a human body. They put me in an Ambervision Perspex box, fearing cross-contamination, and also for purposes of observation. They turned my flesh pages once a day. I've grown since then. I was a board book, originally, one called *Let's Go Shopping!* A little girl in a hat with a trailing, snake-

tongued ribbon, walks down Main Street with a basket over her arm. She buys: sausages at the butcher, oranges at the grocer, a cake at the bakery, and a new pair of shoes at the shoe store.

32   'Leda and the Swan'

33   We were at an aquarium in New England. I think. We never went anywhere else once we moved to NY. Just my mother and my asshole brother, and me, and a lone dolphin in a yellowy pool. We walked around the edge. The whole atmosphere very desultory; yes, I think that's the word I would use.

The Dolphin was playing catch with itself and then with my brother. I wandered around, ten feet back, half wishing to be involved in some way, but already at five I knew that wasn't a possibility. One or the other. My stupid mother. Then The Dolphin threw the ball far, and it landed at my feet. My brother got it and I walked on. He threw it to my feet again. Again, my brother fetched the ball and threw it to The Dolphin. A final time. It landed at my feet. A big beach ball. And my mother looked surprised and smug (as she often did, as if she was directing the whole movie in her head, and in a way she was). She said, she threw it to Nora that time, and I walked close to the pool and dropped the ball on The Dolphin's upturned face. We played for a little while like that. She threw it back. I felt very happy that he (or she, who knows, who cares) wanted to play with me.

34   'Ode on a Grecian Urn'

35   Refers to the Law Hill in Dundee, an extinct volcano, but it looks like a smallish hill.

36   'Last Poem', Ted Berrigan

37   An oblique reference to a Burroughs cut-up.

38   The topic: *Understanding Understanding*.

39   *I Ching*. Hexagram 12, *Standstill*, top changing line. 'You would have been better off if you had relaxed and opened your arms to fate.'

40   That painting is actually called 'The Song of Love'.

41   It was red and said *Christopher Street* on it.

42   'The Waste Land'

43   I think this might be from *Lint*, by Steve Aylett.

44   Poetic license because the Ouse is near Lewes; I hope it bears some relation to the Winterbourne, but even if it doesn't, Virginia Woolf did drown herself in it, in the Ouse that is. But you know that already. For some reason *everybody* knows that. Also this reminds me of the Talking Heads song 'Once in a Lifetime'.

45   Never could understand how anyone ever didn't know
      the earth was round when you can see its curves, at sea,
      when on a hill…

46   'Preludes', T.S. Eliot: 'Wipe your hand across your
      mouth…'

47   It's actually called the Dudhope Roundabout.

48   My use of sign and symbol is roughly coterminous with
      my use of sign and symbol in this book.

49   *Mula Bandha*, a yoga lock.

50   This is a based on a real quote from Kurt Cobain but I
      can't remember what band he was talking about; I believe
      he said, 'are they aware of the fact that they totally
      fucking suck?'.

51   I was thinking of 'The Song of Wandering Aengus' but
      silver trout scales sounded horrendous. It's my favourite
      poem. Yeats.

52   *Gilligan's Island* theme song.

53   Shree Rajneesh. A guru who was popular in the States
      at the time. He was known by some as 'the sex guru',
      according to Wikipedia. These rich kids (not my ma,
      her friends) were followers of his until my mother came
      to visit and then they all got drunk. Or at least that's
      how I remember it. I was only six and could be wrong.

I could be wrong about anything in here. That's why I allowed the reader to shift so much, and the speaker. Who the hell knows what's true when it comes to memories—and also the reader and the writer project so much onto each other, delusion after fantasy after delusion. I find it really touching.

54   A line from *By the Shore*, by Galaxy Craze.

55   This reminds me of Kafka's *Letter to His Father*.

56   *Rosemary's Baby*

57   I'm sure a lot of people say this when they win awards but I remember Lauren Something from the Fugees saying it and I liked her a lot less after that. This was the 90s and I was more judgmental. Lauren Hill.

58   'The Love Song of J. Alfred Prufrock'

59   'Ode on a Grecian Urn', John Keats

60   Ibid.

61   'The World is Too Much With Us', W. Wordsworth

62   Lennon, McCartney

63   This refers back to the keg of solvent Itheherome used to clean the tiles for the keychain.

64 Glenda, never liked her perm.

65 I can't remember what this is from but I can't have
    made it up.

66 *Spinal Tap*

67 Double allusion to Don Paterson and Philip Larkin.

68 'Ode on a Grecian Urn'

69 I was very anaemic when I wrote this poem because I
    had undiagnosed stage 3 colon cancer. They took it
    out and I'm better now.

70 Luce Irigaray's morphology of mucous.

71 It always struck me, that many mid-century psycho-
    analysts, those citing wholly inhumane attachment
    monkey experiments, missed the crucial point that
    attachment is physical; of course it has other attributes,
    and of course physical closeness coupled with sadism,
    neglect, abuse etc. is of no use, and even counter-pro-
    ductive, but, I'd argue, you can't attach successfully
    without touch.

72 Yeats' bee-loud glade.

Epilogue

Why the bazaar? I couldn't figure it out, not as I wrote, not after. I liked the beads; I liked the bombs, and that Itheherome was alone at a stall among deserted stalls. I liked the heat. I clung to the space even though I found it problematic, a little offensive. I didn't know why I was there. Why was Itheherome there.

Then I remembered something I had cut from the poem early on. One day, I was talking to my shrink. I was sitting where I always do, next to a low table, every inch covered with children's toys: dolls, a brimming bowl of marbles, toy soldiers (my shrink always looked slightly put out when I drew attention to them; I think he may dislike children). One doll that always leaned against the wall, in the same spot, was hunched over, doubled up. I made a joke about how he'd maybe endured a bad session with some poor abused kid. When it was time to leave, as I was walking to the door, my shrink casually straightened the doll's hunch. I found this incredibly affecting. Being me, I couldn't 'sit' with the moment, so I asked a question, 'who is he meant to be?' (The doll had a beard and a crown and was wearing a long dress). 'I think a sultan,' you said, noncommittally.

I have never been to a bazaar and have only seen them in films like *Raiders of the Lost Ark* and *The English Patient*. Who am I, I asked myself, as I continued to write the poem, to put my speaker in a place I've never been? The fact that my ancestors were Jews is irrelevant. Why didn't I set it in Riga or Orchard Street? Why didn't I set it at Fairway or Zabar's? A bomb could have gone off in any of those places; it could have been hellishly hot too. I confess, I have never felt more alien than from my own people, than from where I was raised on the Upper West Side, than from my family—but does that excuse the setting? I felt more at ease being a man at times, as the speaker; and that, I allowed, because I am inside me and can make that call, and it changes in here; but as for the place: place is not mine. Still I've left it; I did try to change it, several times. I blame the slouching sultan doll. When it got straightened up I felt a moment of hope like a hole ripped in this real internal landscape. I just want to stress: that was an *imagined* landscape, the outside, like Wonderland.